GIANT graphics

Editor
David E. Carter

Book Design &
Astute Observations
Suzanna M.W. Brown

Giant Graphics
First published in 1999 by HBI,
an imprint of HarperCollins Publishers
10 East 53rd Street
New York, NY 10022-5299

ISBN: 0688-16927-9

Distributed in the U.S. and Canada by
Watson-Guptill Publications
1515 Broadway
New York, NY 10036
Tel: (800) 451-1741
        (732) 363-4511 in NJ, AK, HI
Fax: (732) 363-0338

Distributed throughout the rest of the world by
HBI, an imprint of HarperCollins Publishers
10 East 53rd Street
New York, NY 10022-5299
Fax: (212) 261-6795

All images in this book have been reproduced with the knowledge and prior
consent of the individuals concerned. No responsibility is accepted by producer,
publisher, or printer for any infringement of copyright or otherwise arising from
the contents of this publication. Every effort has been made to ensure that
credits accurately comply with information supplied.

Printed in Hong Kong by Everbest Printing Company through Four Colour
Imports, Louisville, Kentucky.

LOOK! Up in the air...
It's a bird...It's a plane...
It's a BLIMP.

With a logo.

Welcome to the world of advertising, a world in which consumers are literally bombarded with nearly 2,000 commercial messages every day.

For many creative people, the solution to the communications glut is to make the message BIG.

This book is a broad overview of some of the best and most creative examples of what we call Giant Graphics.

This book is meant to inspire you, to turn on the creative faucet in your mind, and to focus it in a slightly different direction. After you finish flipping through these pages, you will never again see a blank building wall or an 18-wheel tractor trailer in exactly the same way.

David E. Carter
Editor

Table of Contents

GIANT graphics

Design Firm
Sayles Graphic Design
Des Moines, Iowa
Designer
John Sayles
Client
Sbemco International

Giant plumbing, with running water, highlights the nonslip feature of Sbemco custom safety floor matting. A visually interesting display was produced in shades of the company's cyan and magenta corporate colors.

Design Firm
Debra Nichols Design
San Francisco, California
Senior Designer
Debra Nichols
Project Manager
Bill Comstock
Designer
Roxanne Malek
Client
California Science Center, Los Angeles

Oversized visuals, reflecting the name of each respective area of the California Science Center, make it easy for the patron to find the way.

Design Firm
David Carter Design Associates
Dallas, Texas
Designers
Cynthia and David Carter
Client
The Palace of the Lost City

An entire environment of sculptural graphics contributes greatly to this resort's image and the visitor's experience.

THE ROYAL BATHS
POOL RULES

NO DIVING

NO INFLATABLE TOYS OR RAFTS
ALLOWED IN POOL

PLEASE WALK IN GENERAL AREAS
OF POOL, NO RUNNING

PLEASE OBEY LIFEGUARD AT ALL
TIMES - FAILURE TO DO SO COULD
RESULT IN INJURY TO YOURSELF
AND OTHERS

CURRY

Design Firm
HKS Inc.
Dallas, Texas
Director of Graphics
Cris Coe
Senior Designer
Nancy Goldburg
Client
Texas Scottish Rite Hospital for Children

Hospitals can be scary places for children, and parents as well. This great signage system creates a friendly air as soon it comes into sight. The juvenilistic style strongly suggests that children are understood in this place—their emotional needs cared for along with their physical ones.

Design Firm
Lippincott & Margulies
New York, New York
Designer
Peter Dixon
Client
Travelers Group

This is a wonderful three-dimensional version of the client's logo, and certainly makes the building easy to find! "You can't miss it..."

Design Firm
Lorenc Design
Atlanta, Georgia
Designers
Jan Lorenc, Karen Webster
Client
CMD Development Chicago

When structures are outside, not only should all views of the object be considered in the design phase, but day and night presentations as well.

Design Firm
**Hornall Anderson
Design Works, Inc.**
Seattle, Washington
Designers
Jack Anderson, Cliff Chung
Client
Seattle Art Museum

Art museums have traditionally been considered by the general public as staid, stuffy environments that were created for the elite. The graphics on these two pages successfully contradict such an attitude with lively images that welcome anyone's presence (or interpretation).

GIANT
graphics

Design Firm
Hornall Anderson Design Works, Inc.
Seattle, Washington
Designers
Jack Anderson, Cliff Chung, David Bates, Mary Hermes
Client
Food Services of America

All the elements of this display lend themselves to the name of the client. Eating utensils refer to food, while southwestern icons have a strongly American identity.

Design Firm
Wilson Sporting Goods
   Chicago, Illinois
Designer
   Mark DesJardins
Client
   Wilson Sporting Goods

Even if you weren't familiar with the company's name, there's no
question as to the product with this off-the-board representation.

Design Firm
Star Tribune
Minneapolis, Minnesota
Designer
Christopher Weber
Client
Star Tribune

A portrayal that extends outside-the-box, and three-dimensional
block letters add visual interest to this billboard.

Design Firm
Thompson & Company
Memphis, Tennessee
Designer
Pat Powell
Copywriter
Lauren Ossolinski
Client
Seabrook Wallcoverings

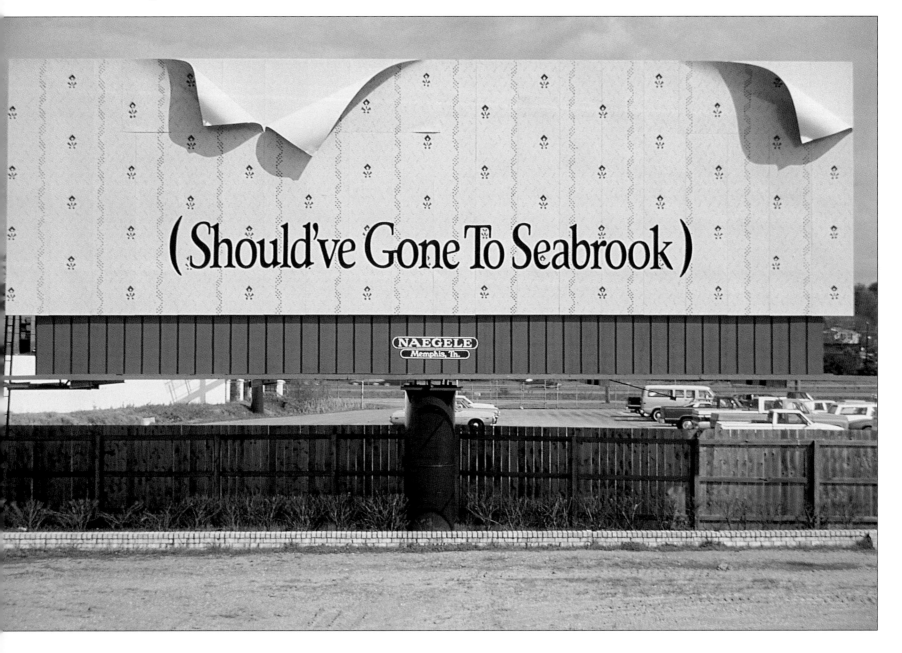

Anyone who's goofed with wallpaper adhesive needs no text to explain this—just the store name where the products can be bought to make it right.

Design Firm
Thompson & Company
Memphis, Tennessee
Art Director
Pat Powell
Copywriter
Lauren Ossolinski
Client
Oakley-Keesee

More than just the car's doors are opened in this visual. The placement of the vehicle, which breaks the boundaries of the billboard, has also "opened" the space, an additional allusion to the headline.

Design Firm
Mithoff Advertising Inc.
El Paso, Texas
Designer
Clive Cochran
Client
Norwest Bank—El Paso

A humorous visual example of the headline makes for memorable
advertising. This design is particularly effective because of the
special consideration of media and environment.

Design Firm
Thompson & Company
Memphis, Tennessee
Art Director & Copywriter
Trace Hallowell
Client
Seabrook

Being able to cover the billboard with a facsimile of the client's product is luck. Being able to recognize the option and execute it is talent.

Design Firm
Sayles Graphic Design
Des Moines, Iowa
Designer
John Sayles
Client
Alphabet Soup

The bold artwork produced by John Sayles lends itself well to
representation on a large surface. This example is especially
eye-catching because it breaks the boundaries of the billboard.

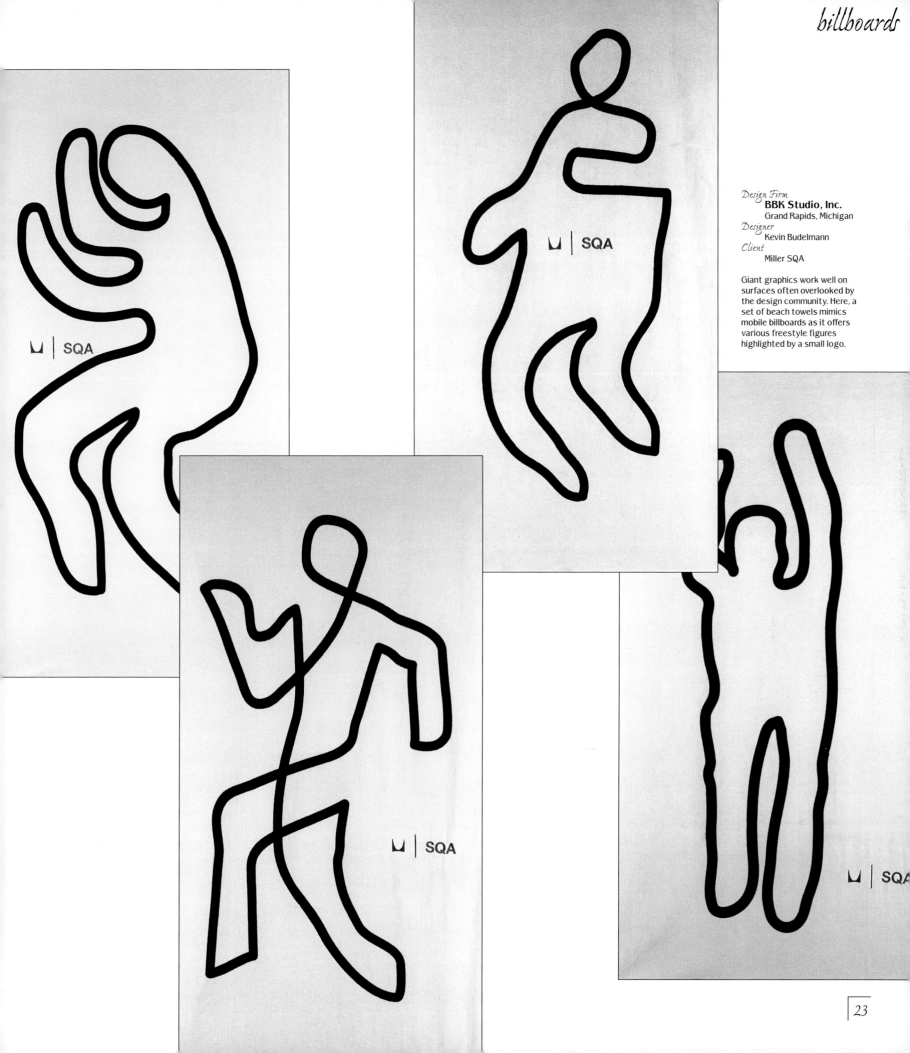

Design Firm
BBK Studio, Inc.
Grand Rapids, Michigan
Designer
Kevin Budelmann
Client
Miller SQA

Giant graphics work well on surfaces often overlooked by the design community. Here, a set of beach towels mimics mobile billboards as it offers various freestyle figures highlighted by a small logo.

Design Firm
Ford & Earl Associates
Troy, Michigan
Designer
M. Francheska Guerrero
Client
Borg-Warner
Automotive

Curved walls create individual space at a trade show, at the same time repeating the shape of many of the automatic transmission parts showcased by the client.

Design Firm
Laura Coe Design
San Diego, California

Designers
Laura Coe Wright, Leanne
Leveillee, Lauren Bruhn,
Denise Heisey

Client
Taylor Made Golf Co.

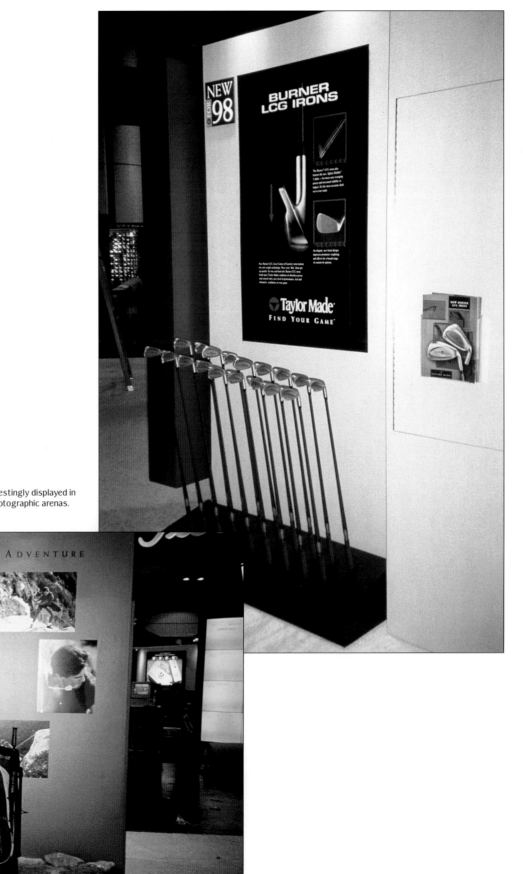

Taylor Made's products are interestingly displayed in accordance with appropriate photographic arenas.

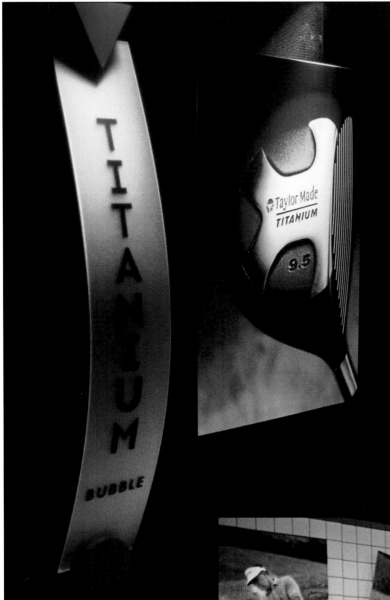

Offering basic information about the products is accomplished by easy-to-read text with lots of visuals.

Design Firm
Hornall Anderson Design Works, Inc.
Seattle, Washington
Designers
Jack Anderson, Cliff Chung
Client
Intermation Corporation

Lots of metal with silver and black colors indicates futuristic, state-of-the art products. Interactive displays appeal to at least twice as many senses as strictly visual displays, and are therefore more memorable.

Design Firm
Gensler
New York, New York
Designers
John Bricker, Anthony DeCaria,
Kamol Prateepmanowong
Client
Haworth

This "Ground Zero Display" not only has a nice integration of text and photos, the
dimensionality creates visual interest on several levels. The lateral extensions leave an
impression of midair suspension. The viewer can walk completely around the work, and
within the display itself, depth is defined by text-printed windows hovering over the art.

Design Firm
Lorenc Design
Atlanta, Georgia
Designers
Jan Lorenc, Chung Youl Yoo,
Steve McCall, Rory Myers
Client
National Science Center

Backlighting creates drama with
a glowing halo.

GIANT *graphics*

Design Firm
Lincoln Park Zoo
Graphics Department
Chicago, Illinois
Designer
Peggy Martin
Illustrator
Linda Bleck
Fabrication
Porcelain Enamel
Client
Lincoln Park Zoo

A Deadly Design

Everything about a lion's skull is designed for hunting, killing and eating large animals such as zebras and wildebeests.

Meet the Skull Behind the Hunter

Large eye sockets face forward for hunting. Like most hunters, the lion's eyes face forward to focus on prey. Prey animals have eyes positioned at the sides of their heads to watch for danger.

Which way do your eyes face?

Three types of teeth help the lion with its kill: **canines** stab and grab prey; **carnassials** cut and shred flesh into bite-sized pieces; **incisors** tear the last bits of meat from bone.

A lion suffocates its prey by clamping its powerful jaws on the victim's throat.

Signage for this outdoor lion and tiger exhibit has fantastic "touch appeal", a major factor in attracting attention to the educational text.

Mystery Cat

We know very little about tigers in the wild. Secretive and solitary, wild tigers live in some of the most remote places on Earth. Scientists need to learn more about wild tigers to save them from extinction.

Tracking a Tiger

For centuries, people tracked tigers by looking for paw prints in the snow or claw marks on trees. Today, new technology makes it easier for scientists to find and study tigers in the wild.

Actual radio collar used for tracking tigers.

Collared
This tiger has been sedated so researchers can attach a radio tracking collar. The collar sends signals that give scientists important information on where and how far the tiger travels.

Design Firm
Wages Design
Atlanta, Georgia
Creative Director
Bob Wages
Designer
Joanna Tak
Client
Fernbank Museum of Natural History

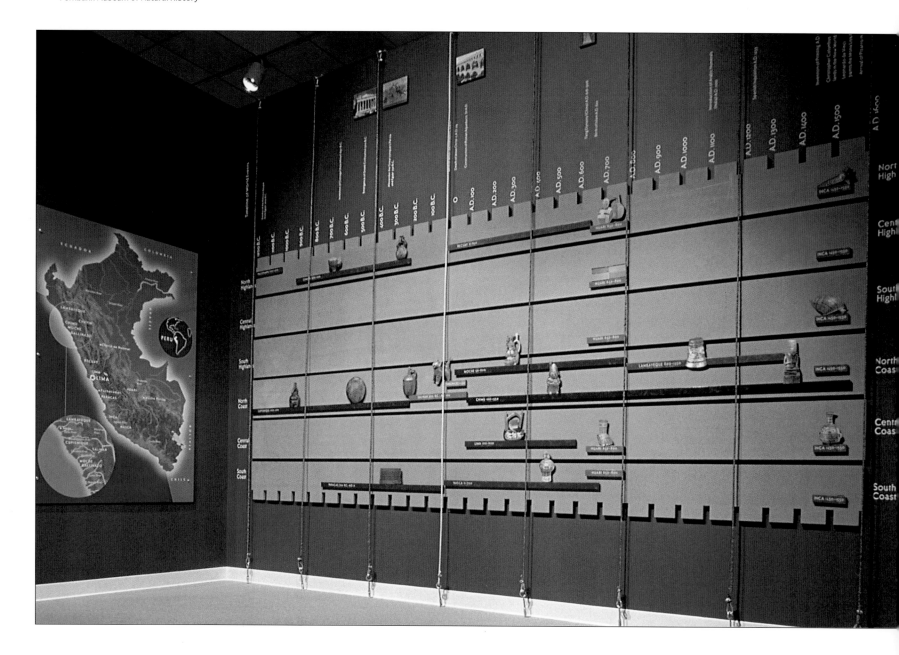

For "The Spirit of Ancient Peru" exhibit, art based on the displayed works was redrawn and incorporated into the environmental design. Well-executed timeline (opposite) compares other world events with the development of Peruvian culture.

The Spirit of

In the Andean region
civilization began over
developed in the varied
culminated in the vast
Spaniards eventually plu
Inca Empire (1438–1554 A.
Chavin, Moche, Nasca, H
of the richest and most
Their cultural achieveme
well-preserved archaeo

Objects from eleven a
2700 years are found
document th

Design Firm
K. Polesky Design
Pittsburgh, Pennsylvania
Creative Director
Paul Selvaggio
(Pittsburgh Zoo)
Designer
Karen Polesky
Illustrator
Dave Klug
Client
Pittsburgh Zoo

White-tailed Deer
Odocoileus virginianus

Deer are mammals with hooves. White-tailed deer get their name from their fluffy white tails, which they raise like flags to signal danger. Deer are fast, graceful runners, reaching 40 mph for short distances.

WHAT DO THEY LOOK LIKE?
- **Weight:** up to 400 lbs.
- **Size:** 34 in. high at shoulder
- **Color:** reddish brown in summer, and gray brown in winter — belly, inner thighs and underside of tail white

WHERE DO THEY LIVE?
In North and Central America, northern parts of South America, mainly forest and woodlands but also swamps in the winter

DID YOU KNOW?
- A male deer is called a buck or stag, a female a doe, and a young deer is a fawn
- Deer can jump 9 ft. in height, 25 ft. in length

WHAT DO THEY EAT?
Deer feed on grass, buds and fresh sprouts, berries, tree bark, acorns and apples.

This signage system collaborates text with photographs, illustrations/paintings, and even some nice clip art. Earth tones in the color scheme create unity, as does the use of unfinished wood mounts for the signs.

Spider Climb

Design Firm
Wages Design
Atlanta, Georgia
Creative Director
Bob Wages
Designers
Randy Allison, Matt Taylor, Joanna Tak,
Rina Motokawa, Vicky Schotte
Client
Fernbank Museum of Natural History

Dependent on the interior architecture of a building, the placement of signs and banners in full view from one area to another invites the patron to advance through the space.

Design Firm
**E Design/Glaxo Wellcome
Creative Services**
Winston-Salem, North Carolina

Designers
Elliot Strunk, Craig O'Brien

Client
Glaxo Wellcome,
customer response center

Repetition of flowing lines originates in the artwork of this display and is carried
through the text treatment for unification. These lines also guide the customer
through the response center with a gentle suggestion of movement.

Design Firm
Belyea Design Alliance
Seattle, Washington
Designer
Ann Buckley
Client
Weyerhaeuser

These displays incorporate samples of the client's paper products. Very
nice arch is filled with a texture of cutaway corrugated cardboard. Notice
the emphasis on upward direction in the architecture, archway, and stepped
displays.

Design Firm
Lorenc Design
Atlanta, Georgia
Designers
Jan Lorenc, Steve McCall,
Chung Yoo, Rory Myers
Client
Lifetime Television

What's better to include in the offices of a television program production company than televisions, television program graphics, televisions, television program descriptions, televisions...?

Lifetime Presents Movies About Women. Featuring Compelling Real-Life Stories, Gripping Dramas, Family Stories, Romances Comedies and Suspense

mystery

comedy

family

Repeating the shape and color of elements within an arena of environmental
design can demonstrate a visual, or even physical, progression.

Design Firm
Kor Group
Boston, Massachusetts
Designers
M.B. Sawyer, Karen Dendy
Client
Waterstone's Booksellers

"Read in order to live."

Flaubert

Gold, black, and white colors used in accordance with a strong emphasis on type are the signature elements that make up Waterstone's signage.

Design Firm
Spagnola + Assoc.
New York, New York

Designers
Tony Spagnola, James Dustin, Robert Callahan

Photographer
Christopher Little

Client
New York Public Library

48

"The quotation wall was designed for the new Science Industry and Business Library, the largest computer library in the world.

"The serpentine wall is nine feet high and 130 feet long, and contains a series of historical quotations on science, industry, and business. The letters are cut-out vinyl, applied to a metallic paint finished wall."

–Tony Spagnola

Design Firm
**Visual
Asylum**
San Diego,
California
Designers
MaeLin &
Amy Jo Levine
Client
Visual Asylum

Consistent use of the not-quite primary color scheme is the strength of this design office's interior. Lots of texture, strong lines, and industrial doors speak directly the firm's name.

Design Firm
Spagnola & Associates
New York, New York
Creative Director
Tony Spagnola
Designers
James Dustin, Robert Callahan

Video Programmer
Advanced Media Concepts
Photographer
Peter Mauss/Esto

Exhibit Manufacturer
Creative Management Services
Client
Lucent Technologies

"The welcome wall at the sales center is made of black glass and is 18' x 9'6". It includes a changeable LED system to welcome customers by name to the sales center. The star background is rear illuminated and also includes over 100 fiber optics to make some of the stars twinkle subtly."

"The video display wall at the sales center is made of black glass and is 19' x 9'6". The silent 12-minute video program (powered by DVD/computer technology) is made up of photographs and graphic imagery that communicate the Lucent message instantly, at a glance, without the use of words."

Lucent
Wireless
Networks

"The customers using the sales center experience brief moments of the program as they move from meeting to meeting within the center."

"The radio wave shape, which is the foundation of
wireless technology, was applied to the front surface
of the glass panels using reflective Scotch®-like vinyl.
The wave shape activates the front surface of the glass
panels and links the eight video monitors together."
—Tony Spagnola

Design Firm
Lorenc Design
Atlanta, Georgia
Designers
Jan Lorenc, Rory Myers, Gary Flesher
Client
Georgia Pacific Atlanta

An industrial display that just doesn't seem to quit is constructed of Georgia Pacific products. Presenting architectural ideas in the form of design and detail, this exhibit is a lot more interesting than some art shows I've attended!

These huge assemblages not only offer
building inspiration, they explain what the
company has to offer, and chronicle its history.

Note the timeline built in the form of a carpenter's ruler.

Don't completely dismiss building products as art media. I
once stretched canvas on a shape I cut from a sheet of
Dow® styrofoam and painted it. I glued it on a larger piece
cut from the same styrofoam, which I had previously
painted with a background texture. (It was pretty good.)

Design Firm
**Hornall Anderson
Design Works, Inc.**
Seattle, Washington
Designers
Jack Anderson, Cliff Chung
Client
Rikki Rikki

Japanese restaurant's name in the form of
chopsticks works very well against the
remaining neon signage.

Design Firm
Visual Asylum
San Diego, California
Designers
MaeLin & Amy Jo Levine
Client
Laser Pacific Environmental Design

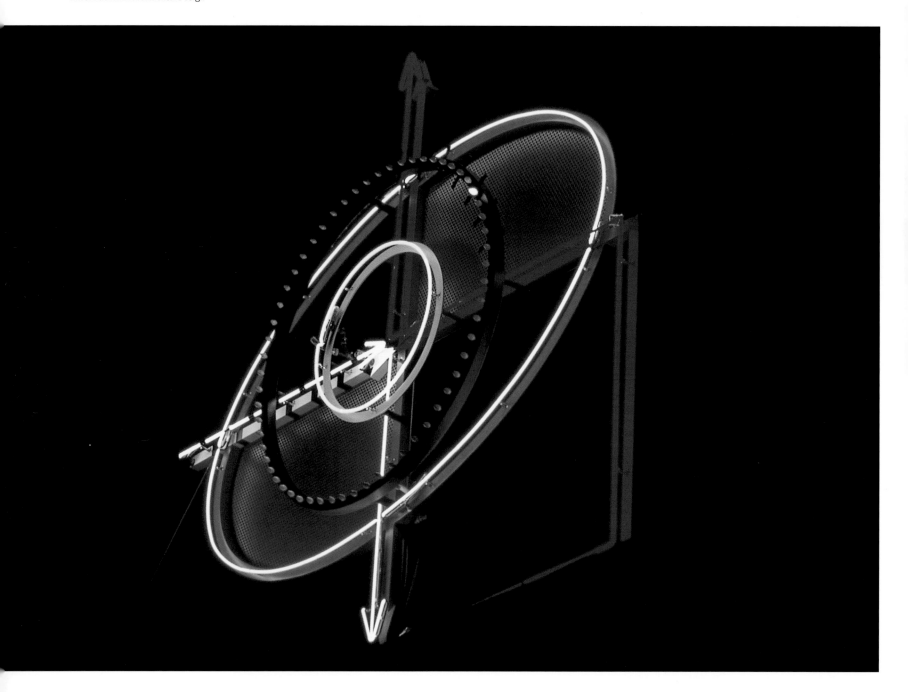

The reiteration of shapes and type style relates three signs from the same system that might otherwise appear as separate entities.

Design Firm
**Kiku Obata
& Company**
St. Louis, Missouri

Designers
Kiku Obata, Chris Mueller,
Rich Nelson, Al Salui,
Tim McGinty, Gen Obata,
Heather Testa

Client
The Museums at
18th and Vine

Neon outlines really define and
add vitality to these characters
and their background.

Design Firm
David Carter Design Assoc.
Dallas, Texas
Designers
Cynthia Carter, Lori B. Wilson
Client
Clicks Billiards

The letters in the name of this sports cafe are connected by the angled path of moving billiard balls. This line also keeps the patron's eye moving toward the right...where there are even larger billiard ball representations.

Design Firm
Graphic Solutions
San Diego, California
Designers
Frank Mando, Ruben Andrews
Client
Donahue Schriber

A very nice intersection of negative space between the shoe silhouette and store name allows the backlighting to become an actual part of the sign. It's also worthy to note that with the use of the icon, there's no need for descriptors to identify what's sold here.

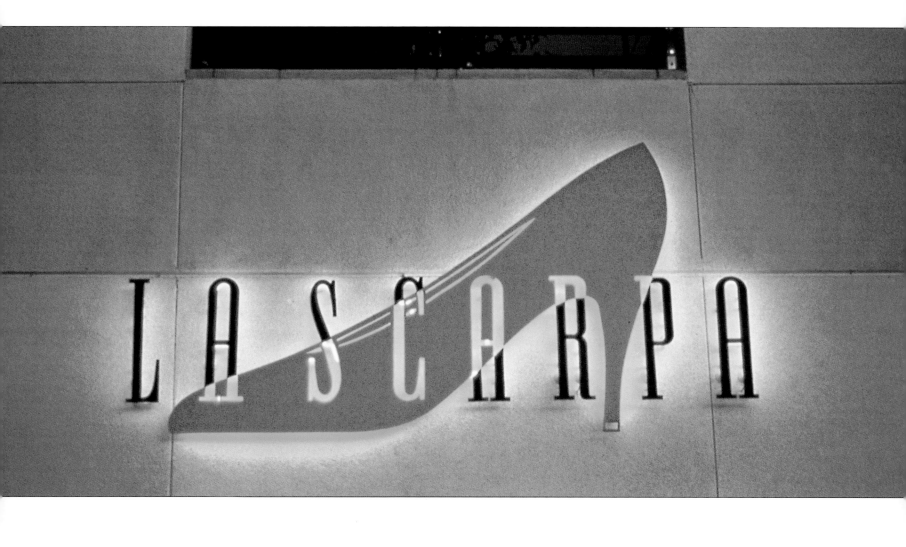

Design Firm
Sayles Graphic Design
Des Moines, Iowa
Designer
John Sayles
Client
801 Steak & Chop House

Bold and very distinctive address numbers
extend from the plane of the door front.
Choosing different sizes allows the numerals
to echo the lines of the door's trim.

Design Firm
Gregory group, inc.
Dallas, Texas
Designer
Jon Gregory
Client
50 Penn Place Shopping Center

Maintaining the same font and a consistent curved line relates these very different kinds of signs.

Design Firm
Sayles Graphic Design
Des Moines, Iowa
Designer
John Sayles
Client
Printing Station

This identifier employs different fonts, registration mark, "paper" image—all printers' tools. Shaped edges also individualize the sign.

Design Firm
Graphic Solutions
San Diego, California
Designers
Frank Mando, Ruben Andrews
Client
Donahue Schriber

Contiguous color scheme in the form of a draped-banner background
works well as the canvas for white letters on the front of this store.

Design Firm
Sayles Graphic Design
Des Moines, Iowa
Designer
John Sayles
Client
Nacho Mammas

Bright colors and abstract alimentary images create the bond between neon sign and awnings in these exterior graphics.

graphics

Design Firm
Graphic Solutions
San Diego, California
Designers
Frank Mando, Ruben Andrews
Client
Donahue Schriber

Not mounted on a typical horizontal base,
curved metal complements the initial letter's
form of this sign and adds a softening element.

Design Firm
Calori & Vanden-Eynden Ltd.
New York, New York
Designers
David Vanden-Eynden, Gina De Benedittis
Client
Valentine Riverside

Striking Valentine-red triangle extending from the negative space in this stone sign develops an interesting play of texture and space.

Design Firm
Tharp Did It
Los Gatos, California
Designers
Mr. Tharp, Jana Heer
Client
Ladbrokes Casino San Pablo

Metal mesh selectively used in the construction of letters in the business
name help continue the curved horizontal lines found in the base of this sign.

Design Firm
**Agnew Moyer
Smith Inc.**
Pittsburgh, Pennsylvania
Designer
Norm Goldberg
Client
The Rubinoff Company

A very strong vertical line is balanced by long angles. It creates a rather casual but unique air.

Washington's Landing

← Waterfront Drive
Marina
Rowing Club
Tennis Courts
Public Park
PARK CLOSES AT DUSK

→ The Village at Washington's Landing

Design Firm
Graphic Solutions
San Diego, California
Designers
Frank Mando,
Ruben Andrews
Client
Donahue Schriber

Broken, colored angles break the boundaries of this sign, adding a sense of movement and vitality.

Design Firm
Anne Gordon Design Pty. Limited
Paddington, Australia
Designer
Anne Gordon

Fabricator
Mr. David Cunneen
(Cunneen & Company Pty. Limited)
Lighting
Mr. Paul Owen
(Lightmoves Pty. Limited)
Client
Darling Walk Retail Arcade

"The brief was to design a sign from the logo to fit within a space 23 meters long. Each letter is 4.5 meters high, utilizing bright eyecatching colors to provide a sense of fun and originality, and attract the attention of passing motorists and pedestrians. Each letter is supported by 'legs' fabricated individually to ensure that the sign aspect and sense of movement varies from every viewpoint. The concept was chosen to interpret the logo in three dimensions and relate to the name of the Arcade.

"Lighting effects give the arcade a spectacular and different image at all times of night and day. The technique was prototyped before fabrication to determine the most efficient spacing of the lamp centers and ensure the best color rendition of each letter through the colored acrylic faces. These are programmed controls for each lighting effect and six lamp circuits within each letter."

—Anne Gordon

Design Firm
Debra Nichols Design
San Francisco, California
Senior Designer
Debra Nichols
Designer
Lynn Paik
Client
Chiron Corporation

This exemplifies a good balance of curves, angles, and straight lines. The bright yellow in the orb is directly repeated in the grid in the background.

Design Firm
Johnson Design Group
  Ada, Michigan
Designers
  Karen Johnson, Dan Carlson
Client
  Johnson Design Group

Fantastic textures and movement in this identifying sign defy
the media from which they are created. A major element looks
fantastically like an industrial-strength paper towel. Script
letters add personality and distinct corporate image.

Design Firm
Sayles Graphic Design
Des Moines, Iowa
Designer
John Sayles
Client
Toscano Ristorante·Bar

Lighting is very important in the presentation of
this version of the sign at night. The name is
unobtrusively spotlighted, while backlighting in
cool colors artfully complements an otherwise
warm color scheme.

Stone texture is used in a visual execution on the restaurant's name logo.

Design Firm
David Carter Design Assoc.
Dallas, Texas
Designers
DCDA staff, Cynthia Carter
Client
Disney Beach & Yacht Club Hotels

Some of the signs in this information system are very individualized. This comes from trying to create an identifier that reflects the specific area of the resort it represents. The more challenging design problem here is to relate the specialized signage with the larger design arena in which it is found.

CAPE MAY
CAFE

There is a successful relationship created across this system with the use of several different techniques.

Shape outlines, bright but slightly subdued colors, off-the-surface or into-the-surface dimensionality, and similar chronological styles pull the single designs into a unity.

Design Firm
Debra Nichols Design
San Francisco, California
Senior Designer
Debra Nichols
Client
Maguire Partners

A 900-acre site, seven million square feet of development certainly provides the space for giant graphics. The complete signage program includes addressing systems, marketing identity and signage, shuttle bus graphics, retail signage standards and design, health club and childcare center signage, and hotel signage.

Abstract animals are eyecatching elements which draw the eye to written information. They are generic icons, equally relative to each of the development's companies.

T.W. King Road
Highway 114 West ←

Sports Club
Sams School Road ↑

Design Firm
**Kiku Obata
& Company**
St. Louis, Missouri
Designers
Kiku Obata,
Tim McGinty AIA,
Heather Testa,
Kay Pangraze,
Patty La Tour,
Jeanna Stoll,
Amy Knopf,
Kathleen Robert
Client
Kiel Center

An appropriate sports theme is carried throughout the seating signage for this indoor arena.

Design Firm
FRCH Design Worldwide (Cincinnati)
Cincinnati, Ohio
Designers
Michael Beeghly, Ray Berberich, Martin Treu
Client
Northwest Plaza

Center Court

◀ Customer Service	Famous Barr ▶
◀ Dillard's	Food Court ▶
▶ JCPenney	JCPenney ▶
◀ Sears	Oshman's Supersports, USA ▶
	Tilt / Cinema ▶

This signage system is full of vitality with bright colors, lots of curves, angled and broken lines .

Notice how the logo elements are translated when they need to fit a perspective other than a flat plane.

The lines of the original could have been lost in this freestanding sign. The solution was to fill some of the negative space with solid colors boasting a large halftone texture.

Design Firm
ASU West/Institutional Advancement
Glendale, Arizona
Illustrator
Simon Silvo
Designer
Geoffrey Boyarsky
Client
ASU West

Emphasizing education and location, warm colors are
used in this depiction of Arizona State University West.

Design Firm
Wolfram Research Inc.
Champaign, Illinois
Designers
Mark Pierce, John Bonadies
Client
Wolfram Research Inc.

Vibrant design consists of art with a strong basis in
mathematics. Not only is the trailer of the MathMobile
painted, the pickup truck is covered in similar form.

Design Firm
Skyline Design Group
Carlsbad, California
Designer
Nanette Newbry
Client
Taylor Made Golf

The design work here makes excellent use
of space restrictions and outline shapes.

Design Firm
Popular Mechanics
New York, New York
Designer
Bryan Canniff
Client
Popular Mechanics

Could there be a more appropriate canvas for this Popular
Mechanics advertising design? The target audience very likely is
composed of those who as children who played with cars and
trucks, now adults who are still fascinated, but by the real thing.

Design Firm
**Hornall Anderson
Design Works, Inc.**
Seattle, Washington
Designers
Jack Anderson,
Heidi Favour, Jani Drewfs
Client
Print NW

Individually-styled initial logos
are used on a fleet of vehicles
for Print NW, each indicative of
the quality of printing offered by
the company.

This kind of treatment has a bonus effect. The similar logos of course create unity and contribute to the corporate identity of the printer, but having each logo noticeably different makes a strong suggestion as to the size of the company. If it's a different logo, it has to be a different truck, right?

Design Firm
Tim Girvin Design, Inc.
Seattle, Washington
Designers
Stephen Pannone, Tim Ferdun
Client
Nalley's Fine Foods

Great tag line for 100% natural peanut butter, "Simply nuts!" The visuals correspond as well: giant peanut butter jars on a bed of nothing but peanuts.

Design Firm
Mires Design, Inc.
San Diego, California
Art Director
José A. Serrano
Designer
Gale Spitzley
Illustrator
Tracy Sabin
Photographer
Chris Wimpey
Client
San Diego Union Tribune

Various media is used to create artworks which, though they have different overt topics, have the same underlying theme. Apparently, the Union Tribune is everywhere.

GIANT
graphics

Design Firm
Platinum Design, Inc.
New York, New York
Art Director
Kathleen Phelps
Designer
Michael Joyce
Client
New York City Police Foundation

NYC "blues" make the background for red and white type.
Really nice fingerprint texture bleeds off the van edge.

Design Firm
Wilson Sporting Goods
Chicago, Illinois
Designer
Mark DesJardins
Client
Wilson Sporting Goods

Despite the immediate impression, the side of a semi is
rarely just a rectangle. This tour truck has three windows
that had to be considered in the execution of the design.

Design Firm
Tim Girvin Design, Inc.
Seattle, Washington
Designers
Stephen Pannone, Tim Ferdun
Client
Nalley's Fine Foods

Companies receive the equivalent of free advertising when they treat their trucks as moving billboards.

Design Firm
Hornall Anderson Design Works, Inc.
Seattle, Washington
Designers
Jack Anderson, David Bates
Client
Capons Rotisserie Chicken

The graphics on this van inform the community that
Capons is not only an eat-in restaurant. They deliver, too.

Design Firm
Watt, Roop & Co.
Cleveland, Ohio
Designer
Kurt R. Roscoe
Illustrator
Javier Romero
Client
AT&T

As this truck houses a traveling display, the exterior
had to be considered somewhat as a storefront. The
curve of the text ribbon creates an archway above
the doorway and highlights the entrance.

Design Firm
Sagmeister Inc.
New York, New York
Designer
Stefan Sagmeister
Client
Studio Motiva

"'Wien in Mode' is a fashion show held yearly in the Museum of Modern Art in Vienna.

"The concept was to dress up the regular Viennese advertising kiosks with actual fabric. The P.R. company responsible for booking the kiosk space for the posters messed up and eight weeks before the show, we found ourselves with no outdoor advertising space. We simply built our own kiosks out of aluminum, polyester and fabric, put them on wheels and hired students to 'drive' them around the pedestrian zones.

"The promotion was featured in most newspapers and made the evening news."
—Stefan Sagmeister

Design Firm
**Hornall Anderson
Design Works, Inc.**
Seattle, Washington
Designers
Jack Anderson, Lisa Cerveny,
Jana Wilson Esser, Nicole Bloss
Client
Best Cellars

The major element in this environmental design is the product itself, perfectly aligned rows of wine bottles. Reflecting the bottles' colors, relatively small descriptor signs possess the same tonal quality.

Design Firm
Sayles Graphic Design
Des Moines, Iowa
Designer
John Sayles
Client
Timbuktuu Coffee Bar

COFFEE TWO
COFFEE 2
COFFEE ONE   TASTE ONE
COFFEE CUP

"Guests are beckoned to Timbuktuu by a sign in the shape of a tree branch, fabricated from plaster and foam. The glass storefront gives passersby a glimpse into the mysterious interior.

"Patron is seated at a tall table Sayles created from steel and wood. The chair backs are painted with a coordinating motif."

"Sayles designed this mural to be a dramatic focal point of Timbuktuu's interior. Graphic icons and tribal masks are recreated in three-dimensional layers of plaster, then backlit for intrigue. The center of this mural showcases different graphic icons and the logo of Timbuktuu."

"BeanArt™ is Timbuktuu's private line of artwork and artifacts for sale to the public. It's also used to decorate the restaurant. Shown here are two posters, screenprinted on flat, Kraft paper feedbags."
—Sheree Clark

Design Firm
FRCH Design
Worldwide
(Cincinnati)
Cincinnati, Ohio
Designers
Michael Beeghly,
John Kennedy, Eric Daniel,
Tim Frame, Sean Davies,
Chris Bolick
Client
Jeepers!

The animal theme of "Jeepers!
Food, fun and a monkey!" is
carried throughout this dining
area with leopard spots and zebra
stripes painted on chair backs.

Notice how all the title signs use text cutouts to add dimension and vitality to the system.

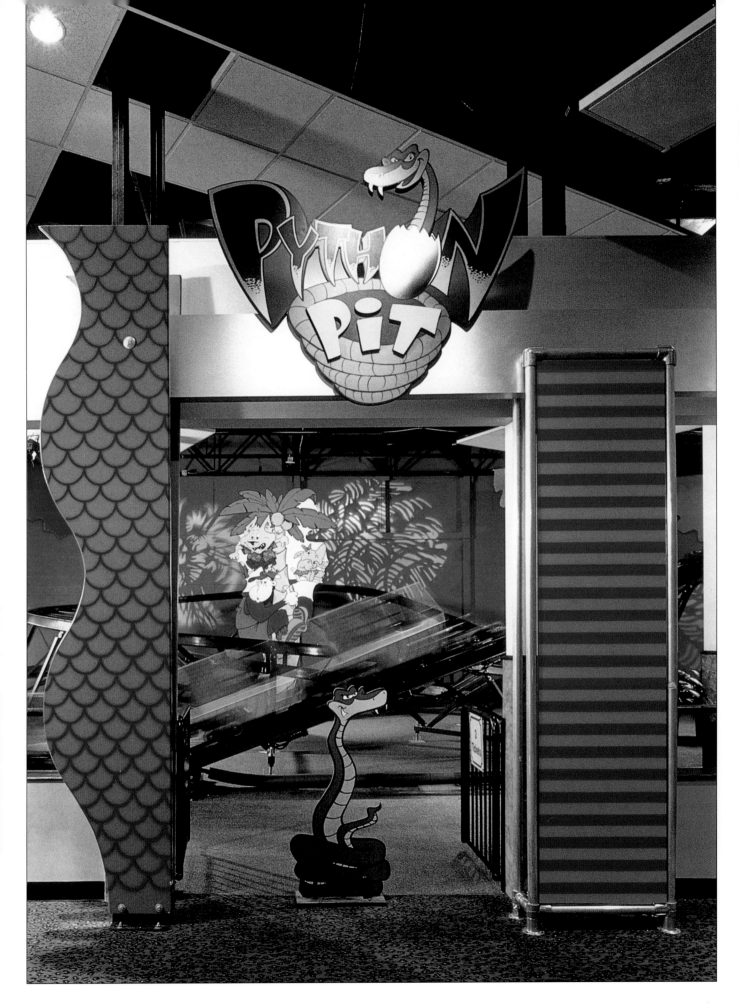

Though a wide variety of colors are incorporated in the signage, one very successful technique that creates consistency is the use of a painted texture in accordance with the area's name i.e. Tarantula Tangle uses spider webs, Python Pit uses snakeskin.

Design Firm
Hornall Anderson Design Works, Inc.
Seattle, Washington
Designers
Jack Anderson, Cliff Chung, David Bates
Client
Smith Sport Optics, Inc.

Sunglasses, this company's specialty, suggest outdoors activities. Lots of things outdoorsy and natural (wood, woodtones, rocks) make a great setting for product display.

graphics

Design Firm
Fitch Inc.
Worthington, Ohio
Creative Director
David Fraser
Project Leader
Phil Wren

Interior Designers
Sara O'Rorke, Krystina Kaczynski, Peter Clayton,
Markham Derbyshire, Hannah Mchallick, Caroline Dibble,
Vicky Stafford, Jackie Latimer, Simon Threadkell
Graphic Designers
Andrew Catlerick, Kenny Laurenson, Shelley Weyman
Client
UCI Cinemas

Reminiscent of art deco design, which enjoyed great popularity during the Golden Age of Hollywood, curved lines are a consistent feature of this movie theater's interior and graphic design.

Design Firm
Hornall Anderson Design Works, Inc.
Seattle, Washington
Designers
Jack Anderson, Cliff Chung, David Bates
Client
Nordstrom Factory Direct

Squares in varying sizes and shades are placed in seemingly random fashion to project liveliness and movement. Darker colors are the background for white letters that indicate the store's different departments.

Design Firm
Fitch Inc.
Worthington, Ohio
Designers
Christian Davies, Randy Miller,
Steve Smith, Paul Lycett,
Jacquie Richmond, Jon Baines,
Kathleen Goode
Client
Chrysler

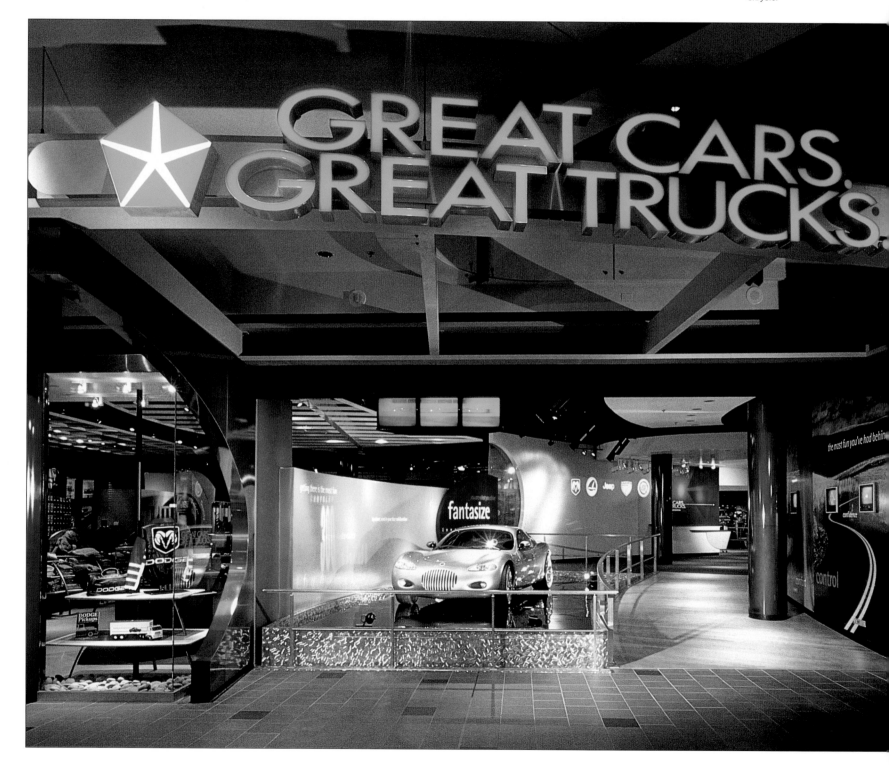

Lots of repeated primary colors and aerodynamic lines give these displays
the in-your-face action of which sports car enthusiasts are so very fond.

Dramatic lighting, shiny surfaces, and minimal text leave the viewer with a series of bold, fast-paced, visual and mental images.

Design Firm
Gensler
New York, New York
Designers
John Bricker, Anthony DeCaria,
Kamol Prateepmanowong
Client
Haworth

The ultimate in using the product as a design element has to be this "product specimen jar." Large in size, but authentic in detail, it even has typewritten observations affixed to the outside of the jar. Red and transparent folding chairs hang on the walls to make an excellent backdrop.

Design Firm
**FRCH Design
Worldwide
(Cincinnati)**
Cincinnati, Ohio

Designers
Paul Lechleiter, Steve
McGowan, Eric Daniel,
Joan Donnelly,
Joanna Huey,
Tracey Lanz

Client
(Carnaval Corner)
Harrah's
Entertainment

Signs and ceiling graphics all take their color cue from the merchandise, bright but natural.

Design Firm
Fitch Inc.
Worthington, Ohio
Designer
Kian Huat Kuan
(retail graphics)
Client
Hush Puppies

Beautiful photographic treatments tie together necessarily different styles of displays.

Design Firm
**Hornall Anderson
Design Works, Inc.**
Seattle, Washington
Designers
Jack Anderson, Julie Lock, Cliff Chung
Client
Starbucks Coffee Company

Without even getting to specific three-dimensional techniques, it's obvious that coffee brown, and the shades and tones thereof, is a corporate color that dominates Starbucks' design.

Design Firm
FRCH Design Worldwide (Cincinnati)
Cincinnati, Ohio
Designers
Paul Lechleiter, Niki Adrian, Eric Daniel
Client
Dick's Clothing & Sporting Goods

A rather subtle employment of backlighting and spotlighting in this signage system makes a huge difference in presentation. Not overly noticeable during use, the lack of lights would greatly fade the signs' presence.

Design Firm
Fitch Inc.
Worthington, Ohio
Designers
Matthew Napoleon, Paul Lechleiter, Mark Artus,
Maribeth Gatchalian, Stuart Naysmith, Fred Goode,
Doug Smith, Jeff Pacione, Fred Weaver,
Ed Chung, Sara DeLeon
Client
Blockbuster

Plexiglass panels reflect light while providing a
transparency that creates an area distinction without
chopping up space.

Design Firm
Fitch Inc.
Worthington, Ohio
Designers
Mark Artus, Bruce Shepherd,
Stuart Hunter, Paul Lycett
Client
Lynx Golf

This Lynx Golf exhibit is actually entered into by the viewer. Once inside, products are displayed by category in perfect geometric form, each against a vertical abstract version of a putting green.

Design Firm
Lorenc Design
Atlanta, Georgia
Designers
Jan Lorenc, Chung Youl Yoo,
Steve McCall, Rory Myers
Client
Donut King

Stripes are repeated everywhere in this environment: menu, floor, ceiling, artwork, maybe even in the soft drink alignment. In contrast, "doughnut shapes" are also found: chairs, tables, artwork, ceiling, products.

Design Firm
Fitch Inc.
Worthington, Ohio
Designers
Matthew Napoleon, Beth Dorsey,
Kelly Mooney, Christian Davies,
Carol Dean, Kian Huat Kuan,
Clint Bova, Doug Smith, Randy Miller
Client
Planet Reebok

This is an example of design that considers the entire space of an environment, floor to ceiling. Monochromatic photos hang from the ceiling, as well as extend off the wall. Curved lines, created in the actual construction of wooden displays, are echoed in the light fixtures and inlaid in the floor.

Design Firm
**FRCH Design Worldwide
(Cincinnati)**
Cincinnati, Ohio
Designers
Paul Lechleiter, Steve McGowan,
Eric Daniel, Tessa Westermeyer
Client
(Art of Gaming)
Harrah's Entertainment

An eclectic selection of art styles from Picasso/Braque to Lichtenstein contributes to this interior's fun atmosphere.

Design Firm
Fitch Inc.
Worthington, Ohio
Designers
Neil Whitehead, Nick Butcher,
Carol Dean, Gabby Barnes, Matt Merrett
Client
Ingredients

Ingredients' graphics are strong in typography, mixing well with baking iconography and actual baking implements such as baker's racks, baskets, etc.

GIANT graphics

Design Firm
Belyea Design Alliance
Seattle, Washington
Designers
Ron Lars Hansen, Christian Salas
Client
Garden Botanika

Free-spirited hearts and hot pink colors are dominant elements in this Valentine's Day promotion.

Design Firm
Visual Asylum
San Diego, California
Designer
Amy Jo Levine
Client
La Quinta Displays

Wrought iron and terra cotta complement a scale
model, art, and blueprints of this Spanish style villa.

GIANT
graphics

Design Firm
**FRCH Design Worldwide
(Cincinnati)**
Cincinnati, Ohio
Designers
Paul Lechleiter, Steve McGowan,
Eric Daniel, Tracey Lanz
Client
(On Stage)
Harrah's Entertainment

Spotlights hanging from metal trusses,
televisions, and entertainment caricatures
are a few of the environmental graphics
employed in the design of this store which
specializes in entertainment merchandise.

Design Firm
UCI Inc
Salt Lake City, Utah
Designer
Ryo Urano
Client
CKSS Associates, Honolulu

This 12' stainless steel kinetic cube is powered by the sun via photo-voltaic batteries.

Design Firm
Gensler
New York, New York
Designers
John Bricker, Lisa Van Zandt, Christian Uhl
Illustrator
Philippe Lardy
Client
The Dime Savings Bank

"Road of Life" mural adds interest to an
otherwise visually-staid work space.

Design Firm
Schlotzsky's, Inc.
Austin, Texas
Designers
Karen Lee, Walt Fleming
Illustrator
Rich Bowman
Client
Schlotzsky's, Inc.

Very nice mural nods at WPA art while modestly suggesting
that Schlotzsky's incorporates whole foods in its menu items.

Design Firm
UCI Inc
Salt Lake City, Utah
Designer
Ryo Urano
Client
Halekulani Corporation

Beautiful glass tile mosaic pool floor is 30' x 30',
and constructed of over a million (!) 3/4" tiles.

GIANT graphics

Design Firm
EDAW, Inc.
Denver, Colorado
Designer
Russ Butler
Client
City and County of Denver

Bronco Banner is separate panels. Each is made to fit within, and be attached to, pre-existing girders to produce one piece of art.

Design Firm
Graphic Solutions
San Diego, California
Designers
Frank Mando, Ruben Andrews
Client
Donahue Schriber

Fun painting makes it simple to remember where the car is parked.

Design Firm
Graphic Solutions
San Diego, California
Designers
Frank Mando, Ruben Andrews
Client
Museum of Contemporary Art

提燈豐商店中國

壽宴　　壽宴

Deep red, black, and dramatic lighting create a mysterious Oriental atmosphere
that hints at a very unusual experience waiting on the other side of the doorway.

Design Firm
Gauger & Silva
San Francisco, California
Designers
Lori Murphy, Laura Levy, David Gauger
Client
Commercial Bank

Quite effective giant dollar bill is draped over the first story's cornice. Corner of the bill aligns perfectly with the ionic column's center, a good move visually, but also a case of form-following-function as the column is one of the points of attachment.

Design Firm
TeleTech
Denver, Colorado
Designer
Christa St. Pierre
Client
TeleTech

Fractured space, distinguished by monochromatic
treatments, has a complicated, Mondrian look.

Design Firm
**Mike Salisbury
Communications**
Marina Del Rey, California
Designer & Art Director
Mike Salisbury
Creative Director
Geoff Thompson
Illustrator
Ray Carbaga
Client
FCB

Larger-than-life, even building-sized advertising makes a strong impact. Consistency in this campaign includes the Levi's red tag and nearly-black-and-white images of people—mostly celebrities—wearing the product. Hmmm...and they're all really **COOL** people, aren't they?

Design Firm
Discovery Design Group
Bethesda, Maryland
Art Director
Dan Cavey
Designers
Dan Cavey, Marta Blanford,
Bill Buttaggi

Photo Editor
Nancy Walz
Client
Animal Planet

A wrapped bus, routed through San Francisco and other
large cities, promotes the cable network, Animal Planet.

Sponsored by Animal Planet and
American Humane Association, this truck
rescues animals from natural disasters.

One-hundred foot wall was covered in vinyl
as an advertisement on Sunset Boulevard
in Hollywood for Animal Planet.

Design Firm
Discovery Design Group
Bethesda, Maryland
Art Director
Chris Doyle
Designers
Chris Doyle, Mike Harris
Photo Editor
Lizebeth Menzies
Client
"Wild Discovery"

Building-sized advertising is an effective way to increase product awareness. The following displays were in Chicago and New York.

Design Firm
Wages Design
Atlanta, Georgia
Creative Director
Bob Wages
Designers
Randy Allison, Joanna Tak,
Kevin Kemmerly, Bob Wages
Client
NationsBank

NationsBank called this campaign "1996 Olympic Presence". It's easy to see that the campaign itself was just that—a presence. Big and bold, it was a reminder, inside and outside, that the Olympics were in town.

Design Firm
Discovery Design Group
Bethesda, Maryland
Art Director
Chris Doyle
Designers
Mike Harris, Richard Howe,
Chris Doyle, Mike Clark
Copywriter
Steve Lance
Photo Editor
Lizebeth Menzies
Client
"Shark Week"

This campaign's goal was to promote
"Shark Week," an annual programming
event on Discovery Channel. Graphics
shown were presented in Los Angeles,
New York, and Chicago

SHARK WEEK
AUGUST 9-15 9PM
Discovery CHANNEL
ELLER
4176
Ed BRAVERMAN Realty
11569
THE T-SHIRT SCREENER STORE
SCREENING & EMBROIDERY
11567
310·826·6000

Design Firm
General Motors Design
Warren, Michigan

Designer
    Joann Kallio
Creative Director
    Larry Faloon
Client
    Birmingham Bloomfield Art Association,
    General Motors Design

Event logo was fabricated as an animated
spotlight on the building's exterior.

Notice the different
effects with a
lighting system that
changes colors.

GIANT
graphics

Design Firm
**Discovery
Design Group**
Bethesda, Maryland
Art Directors
Janet Daniel, Greg Moyer,
John Hite
Designers
Holli Rathman, Jeff
Humberson, Stefan Poulos,
Janet Daniel, Bill Buttaggi,
John Hite, Maryland
Science Center
Illustrator
Martin French
Copywriters
Kathy Smith, Henry Frickel,
Marilyn Bagel, Jeff Simons,
Kelly Monaghan, C.I.
Communications Dept.
Photo Editor
Barbara Henckel
Client
Discovery Channel
Destination Store
Washington, D.C.

Canvas banners, 6' x 8', draw extra
attention to the entrance of
Destination Store.

Pilaster sign is fabricated from rolled steel and etched
with one of four graphic realm icons (kayaker, elephant,
fighter jet, T-Rex dinosaur). It measures 2' square.

Six feet wide and 24 feet long, this mummy banner featured the store opening campaign.

Hot rolled steel vitrine case features laser cut letters.

Table of Contents poster offering the store's highlights and attractions is printed in four color process.

Store directory is constructed of different kinds of steel for subtle but noticeable visual distinctions.

2
Go to know fascinating...
Wander through the art gallery.

TRAVELTOOLSBOOKS
HOMEDECORATION
TOYSGARDENINGMUSIC

M
Dive on famous shipwrecks.
Explore the ocean realm
and take home memories
of its many splendors.

DECORATIVEACCESSORIES
CERAMICSCLOTHINGOUTDOORGEAR
KID'SCLOTHINGTOYSGAMES

1

NATURE DOES NOTHING WITHOUT PURPOSE OR USELESSLY.

WHATEVER YOU CAN DO, OR DREAM YOU CAN,
BEGIN IT. BEGIN IT NOW.
BOLDNESS HAS GENIUS, POWER AND MAGIC

Patinaed slab wall uses sandblasted or
silk-screened, brass-pin mounted letters.

The rotunda that houses the True North Floor Compass
has a totally circular architectural design theme.

The True North Floor Compass is
a multi-layered, five foot circle.

Walls highlighting the B-25 Bomber, the "Workhorse of WWII", are multi-layered and employ 3M graphics.

THE NORTH AMERICAN
B-25
MITCHELL

THE ART OF WAR

B-25s IN THE MOVIES

THE UPS AND DOWNS OF COMBAT PLANES

Black-and-white imagery that's silk-screened on cold-rolled steel
uses pin-mounted letters to convey the history of the B-25 Bomber.

The Hubble Exhibit is a walk-in, interactive one. It
features large-scale Hubble images and storyline.

The multi-layered Conservation International Wall uses wooden-pin mounted letters, canvas graphics, silk-screened letters on glass, and black-and-white mounted images. It features a story on Conservation International's work to preserve biodiversity.

PosterWorks 4.0
for Macintosh and Windows

"PosterWorks 4.0, a large-format production tool for graphic arts professionals, enables its user to compose and print posters, exhibits, and billboards up to 10,000 square feet (1100 square meters) using any PostScript output device.

"In operation, a PosterWorks user composes a large-format layout using either fixed or variable tiles. If variable tiles are required, a custom width and height can be specified for each row and column on the layout. Variable tiles are used, for example, to design a tradeshow display with large main panels and smaller header panels. The PosterWorks user may also vary the margins, overlaps, and gaps between tiles. Artwork is imported in EPS, TIFF, or Scitex format for final sizing, cropping, and placement within PosterWorks."

—Steve Hollinger

This 10' x 8' PosterWorks 4.0 layout precisely matches a TigerMark tradeshow exhibit, panel-for-panel. PosterWorks enables its user to create layouts up to 10,000 square feet, with custom sheet sizes, overlaps, margins, gaps, and bleeds.

This tradeshow exhibit typifies a PosterWorks production job. Panel sizes, and gaps between panels, precisely match the dimensions of the actual TigerMark exhibit frame. The PosterWorks package includes over 200 preformatted popular exhibit, billboard, and signage templates.

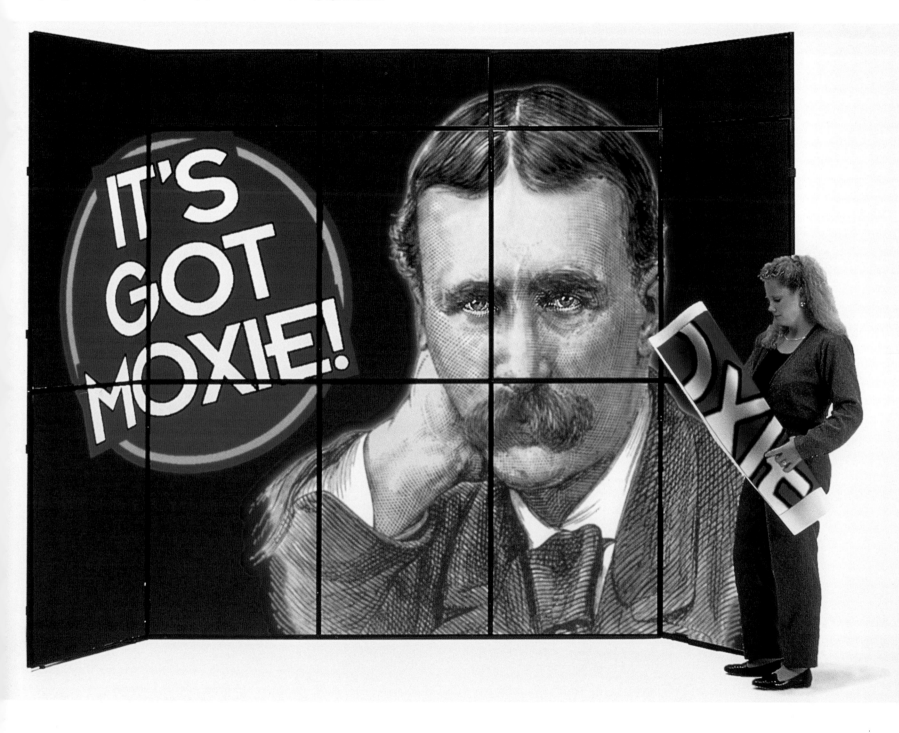

For more information on PosterWorks 4.0, contact S.H. Pierce & Co. at Suite 323, Building 600, One Kendall Square, Cambridge, MA 02139; voice 617.338.2222, or fax 617.338.2223; www.posterworks.com.

index